TOO COOL

Gocart Genius

Phil Kettle
illustrated by Craig Smith

Black Hills

Distributed in
the United States of America
by Pacific Learning
P.O. Box 2723
Huntington Beach, CA
92647-0723

Website:
www.pacificlearning.com

Published by Black Hills
(an imprint of Toocool Rules
Pty Ltd)
PO Box 2073
Fitzroy MDC VIC 3065
Australia
61+3+9419-9406

First published in the United States by Black Hills in 2004.
American editorial by Pacific Learning in 2004.
Text copyright © Phillip Kettle, 2001.
Illustration copyright © Toocool Rules Pty Limited, 2001.

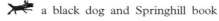 a black dog and Springhill book

Printed in China through Colorcraft Ltd, Hong Kong

ISBN 1 920924 10 8
PL-6202

10 9 8 7 6 5 4 3 2 1   08 07 06 05 04

Contents

Marcy

Dan

Roberto

Toocool

Dog

Simon

Eddie

Chapter 1

Signing Up

Roberto and I were walking through the park, talking about our latest baseball game. Marcy came zooming up on her bike.

"Get out of my way, Toocool, or I'll squash you like a lemon."

1

We leaped off the bike path and into the bushes. Marcy raced past us.

"Toocool, check out the bulletin board," she yelled.

Roberto and I walked over to the board. It said:

Drivers Wanted
TC Park, Gocart Race.

Roberto scribbled his name on the list. Marcy's name was already there. Simon, who was in a wheelchair, said he was the fastest thing on wheels. He said he would win easily.

Dan, who wasn't exactly known for speed, was going to enter, too.

Even Eddie stopped eating long enough to write his name on the list.

I told them all to give up
while they could—I was going
to be a famous race car driver.
I told them this gocart race was
only the beginning of my
amazing racing career.

4

Eddie laughed. "You better stay out of my way, Toocool, or you'll be eating my dust."

"You won't get past the starting line, Eddie," I said.

Eddie almost threw his fruit pie at me, but he changed his mind. He decided it was too good to waste.

I had one week to build the greatest gocart the world had ever seen.

"Come on, Dog," I said. "We're going home to build the world's greatest gocart."

"The second greatest," said Roberto. "Mine will be the best."

"Mine's almost finished," said Marcy, as she rode away. "You two have no hope."

Chapter 2
The Coolest Cart

Everyone hurried home.
I ran straight out to the
workshop. I was thinking
about Marcy. Her gocart was
almost finished. She would have
lots of time to test-drive it.
I would have to get moving if
mine was going to beat hers.

Once I was in the
workshop I felt better. I had
already built many fine pieces
of sporting equipment, so
building a gocart would be easy.

8

It wasn't long before I had piles of stuff all over the floor. I was working at top speed—until a voice yelled over the fence.

"What's all that noise? Can't you do anything that's not noisy?"

It was Mr. Lopez from the house next door.

9

"I'm building a gocart for the big race on Saturday," I told him. "I'm going to win."

"Toocool, when I was your age I built the fastest gocarts on this block."

"Would you help me build my gocart, please?" I said.

"Just be quiet," he grumbled. He knew I'd do fine on my own.

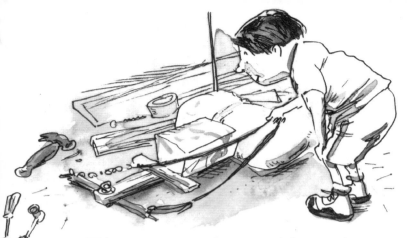

The gocart was taking shape. I covered a cardboard box with tinfoil. It looked like a real motor. Dog's leash made a great steering cord.

Next I strapped an old pillow to the seat for extra comfort. Then I used its pillowcase to make the Toocool flag. I hung the flag from a stick taped to the back.

The gocart looked really cool. All it needed was wheels.

I decided I could do without my old bike. That gave me two wheels. I hadn't seen Mom use her golf bag for a while. That gave me two more wheels.

This was a great gocart. Anyone who thought they could beat me was dreaming. Even Marcy.

The last thing I had to do was paint the gocart. Dad had some red paint that he bought to paint the porch. I decided that red was the best color for a champion's vehicle. I slapped on a few coats.

I had several spills with the paint, but I knew Dad would understand. I was under a lot of pressure.

Chapter 3
A Tense Week

There was one week to go and tension was high in TC Park. Dan started mumbling to himself.

Eddie went home angry after Marcy told him he couldn't eat cake in her gocart.

Simon didn't say much to anyone, but his new T-shirt said *The Fastest Kid On Wheels*.

Roberto and I spent our time walking around the racetrack. I pointed out to Roberto where I planned to pass him. I told him why I was going to win. He took it well.

I went to bed on Friday
night dreaming of the big race.
Dreaming of my victory.
Dreaming of the trophy I was
going to win. Dreaming of my
shiny red gocart.

Chapter 4

A Close Race

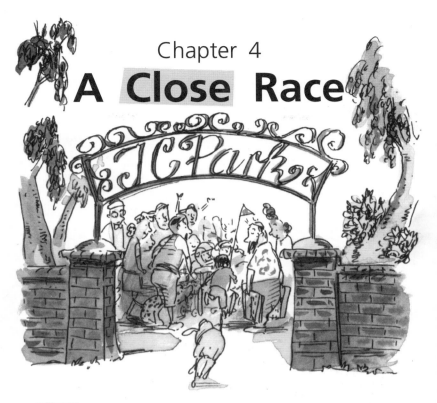

On Saturday morning there was a huge crowd of racing fans at TC Park. They had come to check out the gocarts, but mostly they had come to see Toocool, the Gocart Master, show his driving genius.

I pulled my gocart to the
starting line. I knew it was the
coolest gocart there, but Marcy
said it was a piece of junk.

"Toocool, your gocart is a
piece of junk."

"Drivers, start your engines," yelled Eddie's dad. The sound was deafening as we revved our engines.

I wondered what Mr. Lopez thought of this noise! I looked over at him. He was busy reading the newspaper.

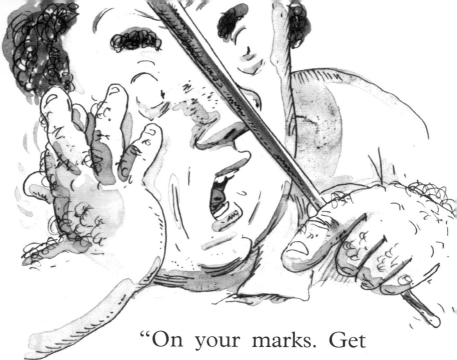

"On your marks. Get
set. Go!" yelled Eddie's dad.

Simon broke away first. He
was in front—until Dog chased
a pigeon across the racetrack.
Simon swerved and his chair hit
the gutter. It bounced into the
air, landed on its wheels, and
kept going. Still, it slowed
Simon down a little bit.

Dan kept to the edge of the racetrack. He was doing okay. It was the first time I'd seen Dan move this fast—ever.

The Toocool machine was working to perfection. I stared ahead. The first speed bump was coming up. It wouldn't be long before I made my winning move.

Eddie hit the speed bump
first. His gocart flew through
the air like a bird, but it landed
like a brick. The four wheels
went in different directions.
Eddie was left sitting in the
middle of the racetrack. I had
to swerve around him.

While that was going on, Marcy made her move. "Out of my way or I'll squash you all like lemons!" she yelled. Simon didn't listen and he nosed in front of her. Roberto stayed right beside me. Dan was right behind us.

It was a close race. There were only 100 yards to go, and one more speed bump to get over.

Chapter 5
Flying Gocarts

We all hit the speed bump at the same time.

My gocart went flying. I hit Simon in mid-air. Simon hit Marcy. Marcy hit Roberto. Dan hit the gutter.

That was the last thing I saw before I shut my eyes.

When I opened my eyes, there were people everywhere. It was like a disaster movie.

Mom was kneeling over me. "Toocool, are you all right?"

"Did I win?" I asked.

Then I heard Eddie's dad. He said the race was canceled. Oh, no! He said there wouldn't be another race until next year.

I walked home, dragging my mangled gocart behind me. Being a champion wasn't always easy. I would have won if the others hadn't been such terrible drivers.

Mr. Lopez stuck his head over the fence. He said he could have beaten me.

"Toocool, if I had been in that race, you would have been eating my dust."

Mr. Lopez is such a dreamer.

I shoved the gocart into the corner of Dad's toolshed. I was through with machines for a while. That gave me an idea. Tomorrow I would give Roberto and Scott a call. It was time for us to start getting in shape for a competition that relied on our own strength.

We were going to enter the Iron-man contest!

The End!

Toocool's
Gocart Glossary

Pit crew—A group of people who take care of your car during the race. The pit crew have to work fast so you can get back in the race.

Sponsors—People who pay you to wear their clothes or their logo. If you are a big star, you get more sponsors.

Swerve—To turn suddenly.

Test-drive—A chance for a driver to see how his or her race car is performing before the real race begins.

Victory—If you have a victory it means you have won.

Toocool's Map
TC Park

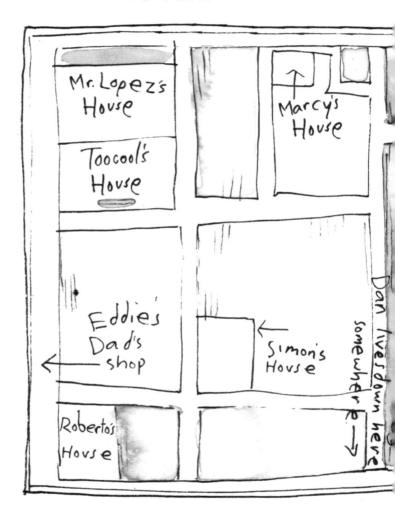

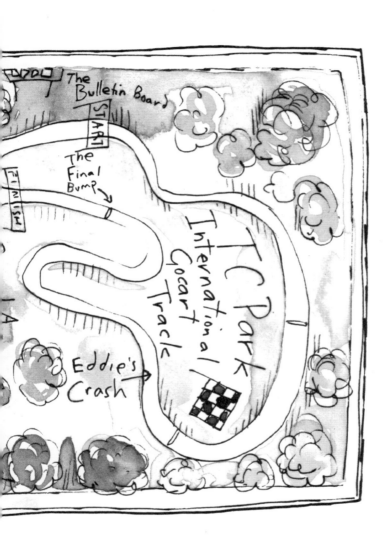

The Bulletin Board

START

The Final Bump →

FINISH

TC Park International Gocart Track

Eddie's Crash →

31

Toocool's Quick Summary
Gocart Racing

Gocart racing started in America in 1956. Today, people in many countries race gocarts. There are many different kinds of gocart races, but the gocarts are almost always small and simple.

People of all ages drive gocarts. There are races for kids who are as young as eight years old. There are also races for adults.

Gocarts have four wheels, and they only hold one person. Gocarts are also very close to the ground, and most of them don't have a roof. Some of them can go more than 120 miles per hour!

Gocart drivers wear the same clothes as race car drivers. They wear a helmet and goggles and a full bodysuit. They look really cool.

Many race car drivers start out driving gocarts.

The **Gocart**

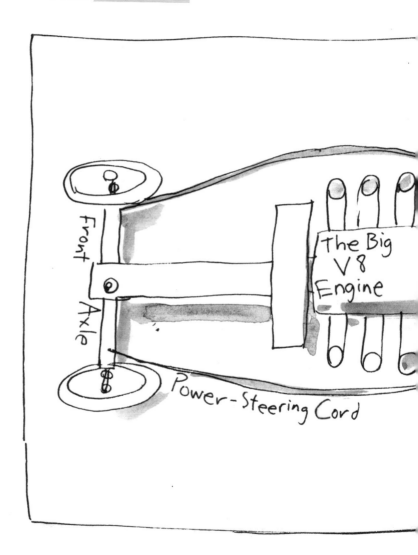

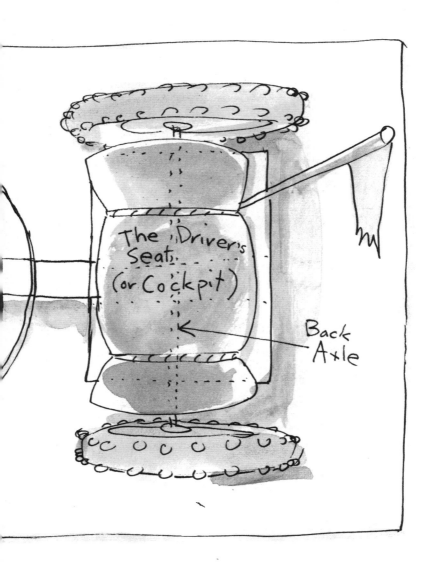

The Driver's Seat (or Cockpit)

Back Axle

Q & A with Toocool
He Answers His Own Questions

What are the best kind of wheels for a gocart?

The best wheels are the ones that don't cost anything. Wheels from an old stroller are good. Some old lawn mowers have great wheels. Don't take wheels from your sister's bike, though. She won't be too happy.

How long have you been interested in gocarts?

I've always loved gocarts. It started when I was a baby. I remember sitting in my stroller and thinking what a great gocart it would make.

Should you take passengers in your gocart?

I think it would be a great idea, but every time I ask someone to come for a ride, they say no. Even when I ask Dog, he runs away. So maybe it's not a good idea.

Do gocarts have a radio?

No way! You wouldn't be able to hear it. Gocart motors are very loud.

Do you always wear a helmet in your gocart?

Yes. I have a special helmet for racing. It has stickers. I have many sponsors. They like to see a champion wear their stickers.

Have you and your gocart ever been on television?

Yes. Most of the races I have been in have been on TV, but I never get to see them because I'm racing. Racing is always shown live from the racetrack.

When do you think you will be in Formula One racing?

It won't be long. I just have to grow a little. I can almost reach the pedals in a race car.

I can already see over the steering wheel. I will probably be the youngest race car driver ever.

Who will be in your pit crew?

Most of my friends want to be in my pit crew. They always say, "Toocool, we want to be in your pit crew." I'm not sure how many people are allowed in a pit crew. I think the best drivers have the biggest pit crews.

Gocart Quiz
How Much Do You Know about Gocart Racing?

Q1 What side of the track should you race on?

A. The left side. *B.* The right side. *C.* Either side.

Q2 Do gocart drivers wear seatbelts?

A. Always. *B.* When they remember. *C.* No.

Q3 How much gasoline does a gocart like Toocool's use?
A. Gallons. *B.* None.
C. A spoonful.

Q4 What color are the fastest gocarts?
A. Red. *B.* White. *C.* Brown.

Q5 What does a pit crew do?
A. Repairs and refueling.
B. Yell at the driver.
C. Tow the gocart away.

Q6 When do gocart drivers wear a helmet?
A. Whenever they are in the gocart. *B.* When they forget their sunscreen. *C.* When it's cold.

Q7 If you took two wheels off your gocart, what would it do?
A. Stop. **B.** Crash. **C.** Go faster.

Q8 If you saw Toocool in his gocart, what would you do?
A. Cheer. **B.** Ask for a ride.
C. Find somewhere to hide.

Q9 Which is the fastest?
A. Race car. **B.** Racehorse.
C. Toocool's gocart.

Q10 Who will be the next world champion race car driver?
A. Marcy. **B.** Eddie. **C.** Toocool.

ANSWERS

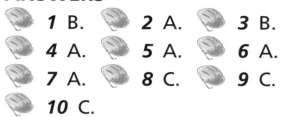

1 B. **2** A. **3** B.
4 A. **5** A. **6** A.
7 A. **8** C. **9** C.
10 C.

If you got ten questions right, you are almost ready to race. If you got more than five right, stay on your bike a little longer. If you got fewer than five right, you should keep walking.

TOOCOOL

Invincible Iron Man

The iron-man contest is a tough event. Will rock-hard muscles and legs of steel be all **Toocool** needs to win?

Titles in the Toocool series